But what is happiness
except the simple harmony
between a man and
the life he leads.

ALBERT CAMUS

To

From

Also by Barbara Milo Ohrbach

Love *Your* Life

MAKING THE MOST OF EACH DAY

Barbara Milo Ohrbach

Clarkson Potter/Publishers
New York

Published by Clarkson Potter/Publishers, New York, New York
Member of the Crown Publishing Group, a division of
Random House, Inc.
www.randomhouse.com

CLARKSON N. POTTER is a trademark and POTTER and
colophon are registered trademarks of Random House, Inc.

Printed in the United States of America

Design by Jan Derevjanik

Library of Congress Cataloging-in-Publication Data
Love your life : making the most of each day /
[compiled] by Barbara Milo Ohrbach.—1st ed.
1. Conduct of life—Quotations, maxims, etc.
I. Ohrbach, Barbara Milo.
PN6084.C556 L68 2002
082—dc21   2001057804

ISBN 0-609-80924-5
10 9 8 7 6 5 4 3 2 1
First Edition

Count Your Blessing . . .

I should have . . . I could have . . . why didn't I . . . what if . . . Nothing seems to measure up, even when we have everything we thought we wanted. The more we chase contentment, the more elusive it becomes. Why do so many of us seem dissatisfied?

Being happy is really not all that complicated, even when large events overtake us and force us to examine our priorities. Instead of expecting "to have it all," perhaps it's time to rediscover the basic values and small blessings that really make our lives beautiful. The number of sunsets we see each year is how one person put it recently.

Once you start to think hard about what matters, you realize that *each day* is the gift: having the time to spend with people you care about; cultivating contentment and spirituality within yourself; sharing with others; finding joy

5

in a simpler life; and remembering to always look at the world around you with gratitude.

Ralph Waldo Emerson once said: "I am thankful for small mercies. I compared notes with one of my friends who expects everything of the universe, and is disappointed when anything is less than the best, and I found that I begin at the other extreme, expect nothing, and I am always full of thanks for moderate goods." Sound advice!

So shouldn't we try to look on the bright side? Life really is beautiful. Even though we all have struggles to overcome and challenges to meet, we can try to make it a habit to appreciate how lucky we are. This gem by Henry David Thoreau is pinned above my desk. It reminds me to stop complaining about silly things and to count my many blessings.

> *However mean your life is, meet it and live it; do not shun and call it hard names. It is not so bad as you are. It looks poorest when you are richest. The fault-finder will find faults even in paradise. Love your life.*

Barbara Milo Ohrbach

Life loves to be taken by the lapel and be told:
"I am with you, kid. Let's go."
MAYA ANGELOU

Leap, and the net will appear.
JULIA CAMERON

I wake each morning with the thrill of
expectation and the joy of being truly alive.
And I'm thankful for this day.
ANGELA L. WOZNIAK

Fear less, hope more;
Whine less, breathe more;
Hate less, love more;
And all good things are yours.
SWEDISH PROVERB

Hop

Life is just a bowl of cherries.

ANONYMOUS

Miracles happen to those who believe in them.

BERNARD BERENSON

It is only with the heart that one can see rightly;

what is essential is invisible to the eye.

ANTOINE DE SAINT-EXUPÉRY

If you cannot find the truth right where you are,
where else do you expect to find it?

MASTER DOGEN

You must learn day by day, year by year,
to broaden your horizon. The more things you love,
the more you are interested in, the more you enjoy,
the more you are indignant about—the more
you have left when anything happens.

ETHEL BARRYMORE

There is symbolic as well as actual beauty in the
migration of the birds, the ebb and flow of the tides,
the folded bud ready for the spring.

RACHEL CARSON

Every problem has a gift for you in its hands.
RICHARD BACH

Love God and do what you will.

ST. AUGUSTINE

Knock on the sky and listen to the sound!

ZEN SAYING

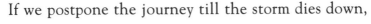

If we postpone the journey till the storm dies down,

we may never get started.

J. I. PACKER

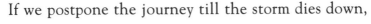

There is no sadder sight than a young pessimist.

MARK TWAIN

I beg you . . . to have patience with everything unresolved in your heart and try to love the questions themselves as if they were locked rooms or books written in a very foreign language. Don't search for the answers, which could not be given you now, because you would not be able to live them. And the point is, to live everything. Live the questions now. Perhaps then, someday far in the future, you will gradually, without ever noticing it, live your way into the answer.

RAINER MARIA RILKE

This is the best day the world has ever seen.

Tomorrow will be better.

R. A. CAMBELL

To look for the best and see the beautiful is the

way to get the best out of life each day.

LINCOLN STEFFENS

All our lives we are preparing to be something

or somebody, even if we don't know it.

KATHERINE ANNE PORTER

The only true security in life comes

from relishing life's insecurity.

M. SCOTT PECK

Simp

There must be more to life than
having everything.

MAURICE SENDAK

Take the gentle path.

GEORGE HERBERT

lifying

Consciously cultivate the ordinary.

WALKER PERCY

People exaggerate the value of things they haven't got.

GEORGE BERNARD SHAW

I'd rather have roses on my table than
diamonds on my neck.

EMMA GOLDMAN

Life isn't a matter of milestones, but of moments.

ROSE KENNEDY

To sit in the shade on a fine day and look upon
verdure is the most perfect refreshment.

JANE AUSTEN

If only I may grow: firmer, simpler—quieter, warmer.

DAG HAMMARSKJÖLD

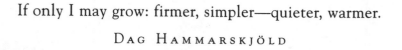

When we recall the past, we usually find that it is the simplest things—not the great occasions—that in retrospect give off the greatest flow of happiness.

BOB HOPE

One cannot collect all the beautiful shells on the beach. One can collect only a few, and they are more beautiful if they are few.

ANNE MORROW LINDBERGH

It is perhaps a more fortunate destiny to have a taste for collecting shells than to be born a millionaire.

ROBERT LOUIS STEVENSON

I actually just love being. As you get older it
behooves you to spend the time being true to yourself.

JOANNE WOODWARD

If it were possible to simplify life to the utmost,
how little one really wants!

GERTRUDE JEKYLL

If my heart can become pure and simple like
that of a child, I think there probably can be
no greater happiness than this.

KITARO NISHIDA

A morning-glory at my window satisfies
me more than the metaphysics of books.

WALT WHITMAN

People always ask me how could I remember
so much. I think I had an easy path back into
the past because when I was growing up we had
nothing. So we had to manufacture our own
days, and our lives were very uncluttered.

FRANK McCOURT

Teach us delight in simple things.

RUDYARD KIPLING

Watch in the spring sunshine the stockbroker
and the great barrister going indoors to make
money and more money and more money when
it is a fact that five hundred pounds a year
will keep one alive in the sunshine.

VIRGINIA WOOLF

D

Do what you can where you are
with what you've got.

THEODORE ROOSEVELT

You should not confuse your career with your life.

DAVE BARRY

oing

A happy life is one spent in learning,
earning, and yearning.

LILLIAN GISH

As long as you're doing something interesting
and good, you're in business.

LOUIS ARMSTRONG

I'm a great believer in luck, and I find the
harder I work, the more luck I have.

THOMAS JEFFERSON

Your talent is God's gift to you.
What you do with it is your gift back to God.

LEO BUSCAGLIA

I want to do it because I want to do it. Women must
try to do things as men have tried. When they fail,
their failure must be but a challenge to others.

AMELIA EARHART

Great things are not done by impulse,
but by a series of small things brought together.

VINCENT VAN GOGH

There is as much dignity in plowing a field
as in writing a poem.

BOOKER T. WASHINGTON

Life engenders life. Energy creates energy.
It is by spending oneself that one becomes rich.

SARAH BERNHARDT

The only way to enjoy anything in this life is to earn it first.

GINGER ROGERS

If a man does his best, what else is there?

GENERAL GEORGE S. PATTON

I really think that the growth inside of you
is there for you to water. And it doesn't mean
you have to be a successful actor or director.
You can really be successful starting to read,
starting to learn, starting to do a lot of things . . .
it has to do with you as a person.

LIV ULLMANN

It is the way of disappointment to expect too
much, or only to work or only to play. So you
have to lower your expectations, hope for the
best and work and play. The dictionary definitions
of *work* and *play* have much in common, as if the
person defining these words could not pull them
apart to be two separate things.

SISTER MARY CORITA KENT

Each of us has unique interests, skills, and talents, and it is when we act from our hearts, with our minds, through our hands that we are most satisfied and effective.

JIMMY CARTER

All my life I've been working on the work—
every canvas a sentence or paragraph of it.

ROBERT MOTHERWELL

You've achieved success in your field when you don't know whether what you're doing is work or play.

WARREN BEATTY

I'm a tough old turkey. My legs aren't very good anymore, but otherwise I'm in very good health and I love my work.

JULIA CHILD

Be

Believe in yourself! Have faith in your abilities!

NORMAN VINCENT PEALE

Become so wrapped up in something
that you forget to be afraid.

LADY BIRD JOHNSON

lieving

I have found that if you love life, life will love you back.

ARTHUR RUBINSTEIN

A sheltered life can be a daring life as well,
for all serious daring starts from within.

EUDORA WELTY

Any idiot can face a crisis—it's this day-to-day
living that wears you out.

ANTON CHEKHOV

I get up. I walk. I fall down. Meanwhile, I keep dancing.

HILLEL THE ELDER

I refuse to believe that trading recipes is silly.
Tuna fish casserole is at least as real as corporate stock.

BARBARA GRIZZUTI HARRISON

It is possible to be different and still be all right.

ANNE WILSON SCHAEF

Self-reliance and self-respect are about as valuable commodities as we can carry in our pack through life.

LUTHER BURBANK

Keep your fears to yourself, but share your courage with others.

ROBERT LOUIS STEVENSON

Life is either a daring adventure or it is nothing.

HELEN KELLER

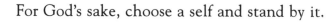

For God's sake, choose a self and stand by it.

WILLIAM JAMFS

So whatever you do, just do it. Do not worry about making a fool of yourself. Making a damn fool of yourself is absolutely essential. And you will have a great time.

GLORIA STEINEM

When we can begin to take our failures non-seriously, it means we are ceasing to be afraid of them. It is of immense importance to learn to laugh at ourselves.

KATHERINE MANSFIELD

I find that when we really love and accept and approve of ourselves as we are, then everything in life works.

LOUISE HAY

I happen to enjoy an element of adventure and danger. I think that if you occasionally live dangerously it helps you appreciate life. Not only that, you discover your own abilities which, perhaps, you did not know were there.

PRINCE CHARLES

Life is 10 percent what you make it and 90 percent how you take it.

IRVING BERLIN

To the question of your life, you are the only answer. To the problems of your life, you are the only solution.

JO COUDERT

Sha

Let no one come to you without
leaving better and happier.

MOTHER TERESA

Let us be grateful to people who make us happy;
they are the charming gardeners who
make our souls blossom.

MARCEL PROUST

ring

We must love friends for their sake rather than our own.

CHARLOTTE BRONTË

What do we live for if not to make life
less difficult to each other.

GEORGE ELIOT

No act of kindness, no matter how small, is ever wasted.

AESOP

It is one of the most beautiful compensations
of life that no man can sincerely try to help
another without helping himself.

RALPH WALDO EMERSON

We make a living by what we get,
but we make a life by what we give.

WINSTON CHURCHILL

Years and years of happiness only make us realize
how lucky we are to have friends that have
shared and made that happiness a reality.

ROBERT E. FREDERICK

One can never speak enough of the virtues,
the dangers, the power of shared laughter.

FRANÇOISE SAGAN

All that lasts in this world is what you pass on—
the rest is smoke and mirrors.

STEPHEN KING

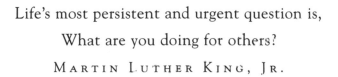

Life's most persistent and urgent question is,
What are you doing for others?

MARTIN LUTHER KING, JR.

For I have learned the truth: there are greater
pursuits than self-seeking. Glory is not a conceit.
It is not a decoration for valor. It is not a prize
for being the most clever, the strongest, or the
boldest. Glory belongs to the act of being constant
to something greater than yourself, to a cause, to
your principles, to the people on whom you rely,
and who rely on you in return. No misfortune,
no injury, no humiliation can destroy it.

SENATOR JOHN MCCAIN

Three things in human life are important:
The first is to be kind. The second is to be kind.
The third is to be kind.

HENRY JAMES

Do all the good you can, in all the ways you can, in all the places you can, at all the times you can, to all the people you can, as long as ever you can.

JOHN WESLEY

The opera reminds me to live well and share it.

JOSEPH KRENUS, METROPOLITAN OPERA USHER

The older I get, the greater power I seem to have to help the world; I am like a snowball— the further I am rolled, the more I gain.

SUSAN B. ANTHONY

Accept what people offer. Drink their milkshakes. Take their love.

WALLY LAMB

Lau

A smile increases your face value.
SIGN IN A LONDON SHOP

Happiness is good health and a bad memory.

INGRID BERGMAN

ghing

You grow up the day you have your first
real laugh at yourself.

ETHEL BARRYMORE

Find something to laugh about.

SEBASTINE CHAMFORT... MAYA ANGELOU

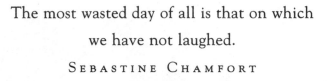

Those who want to have some fun out of life, do.

MALCOLM FORBES

The most wasted day of all is that on which
we have not laughed.

SEBASTINE CHAMFORT

And if I had roses all the way, would I recognise
it at the time? How often do people look back and say,
"That was the great time for me and I didn't know it."

SIR BOB GELDOF

There is only one happiness in life, to love and be loved.

GEORGE SAND

You're happiest while you're making
the greatest contribution.

ROBERT F. KENNEDY

If you want to be happy, be.

ALEKSEY TOLSTOY

Happiness makes up in height for what it lacks in length.

ROBERT FROST

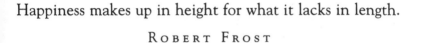

Make the coming hour overflow with joy,
and let pleasure drown in the brim.

WILLIAM SHAKESPEARE

Money cannot buy sunsets, singing birds,
and the music of the wind in the trees.

GEORGE HORACE LORIMER

The greater part of our happiness depends on our disposition and not our circumstances.

MARTHA WASHINGTON

Happiness doesn't depend upon who you are or what you have; it depends solely upon what you think.

DALE CARNEGIE

We all live with the objective of being happy; our lives are all different and yet the same.

ANNE FRANK

The longer I live the more beautiful life becomes.

FRANK LLOYD WRIGHT

It is neither wealth nor splendor, but tranquility and occupation which give happiness.

THOMAS JEFFERSON

Even a happy life cannot be without a measure of darkness, and the word "happy" would lose its meaning if it were not balanced by sadness. It is far better to take things as they come along with patience and equanimity.

CARL JUNG

The older I got, the heavier my burden of not having been happy yet.

NUALA O'FAOLAIN

Oh, I've never had the knack of knowing I was happy right while the happiness was going on.

ANNE TYLER

Suc

I don't know the secret to success, but the
key to failure is to try and please everyone!

BILL COSBY

Try not to become a man of success
but rather try to become a man of value.

ALBERT EINSTEIN

ceeding

Life is a succession of moments.
To live each one is to succeed.

SISTER MARY CORITA KENT

Success is a . . . trendy word. Don't aim for success if you want it; just do what you love and it will come naturally.

DAVID FROST

It wasn't about money. It was about happiness.

TIGER WOODS

You only live once—but if you work it right, once is enough.

JOE E. LEWIS

What's money? A man is a success if he gets up
in the morning and goes to bed at night
and in the middle does what he wants to do.

BOB DYLAN

What really matters is what you do with what you have.

SHIRLEY LORD

Most people would succeed in small things,
if they were not troubled with great ambitions.

HENRY WADSWORTH LONGFELLOW

Fame is a bee.

It has a song—

It has a sting—

Ah, too, it has a wing.

EMILY DICKINSON

Failure isn't so bad if it doesn't attack the heart.

Success is all right if it doesn't go to the head.

GRANTLAND RICE

I always wanted to be a star—

I'm not gonna bitch about it now.

DOLLY PARTON

What matters is how you choose to love.
As you know, there's a lot of emphasis placed
on success, and I hear it all the time.
But what I know is there is no success where
there is no joy, so instead of looking for success
in your life, look for the thing that is
going to bring you the greatest joy.
Joy is the only goal really worth seeking.

OPRAH WINFREY

As long as you did the very best that you
were able to do, then that was what you were
put here to do and that was what you were
accomplishing by being here.

ELEANOR ROOSEVELT

We judge ourselves by what we feel capable of doing,
while others judge us by what we have already done.

HENRY WADSWORTH LONGFELLOW

I have not failed. I've just found 10,000 ways that won't work.

THOMAS EDISON

Success isn't measured by the position you reach in life;
it's measured by the obstacles you overcome.

BOOKER T. WASHINGTON

The secret of success is this: there is no secret of success.

ELBERT HUBBARD

Character consists of what you do on the
third and fourth tries.

JAMES A. MICHENER

Dre

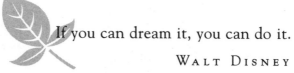

If you can dream it, you can do it.

WALT DISNEY

It is astonishing how short a time it takes
for very wonderful things to happen.

FRANCES HODGSON BURNETT

Just when the caterpillar thought the world was over,
it became a butterfly.

ANONYMOUS

To begin again. To begin again. To begin again.

COLETTE, AT 79

It ain't as bad as you think. It will look better
in the morning.

COLIN POWELL

Each day, look for a kernel of excitement.

BARBARA JORDAN

Thinking is more interesting than knowing,
but less interesting than looking.

GOETHE

To be blind is bad, but worse it is to have eyes
and not to see.

HELEN KELLER

My favorite thing is to go where I've never been.

DIANE ARBUS

My challenge was not to do the impossible—but to
learn to live with the possible.

SUE BENDER

Life just is. You have to flow with it. Give yourself to
the moment. Let it happen.

JERRY BROWN

The real voyage of discovery consists not in seeking
new landscapes but in having new eyes.

MARCEL PROUST

I've never been poor, only broke. Being poor is a frame
of mind. Being broke is only a temporary situation.

MIKE TODD

Each day the first day: Each day a life.

DAG HAMMARSKJÖLD

Just don't give up trying to do what you really want
to do . . . . Where there's love and inspiration,
I don't think you can go wrong.

ELLA FITZGERALD

The human mind cannot hold two opposing thoughts at
the same time. So, if you hold a positive thought, you
cannot hold a negative one.

LILY TOMLIN

You've got to follow your passion. You've got to figure out
what it is you love—who you really are. And have the
courage to do that. I believe that the only courage anybody
ever needs is the courage to follow your own dreams.

OPRAH WINFREY

When I was in my early 20s, I didn't know
what tomorrow would bring. Now starting at 40,
I still don't know—and that's what makes
this life exciting. So map out your future,
but do it in pencil.

JON BON JOVI

Three rules of work
1. Out of clutter, find simplicity.
2. From discord, find harmony.
3. In the middle of difficulty lies opportunity.

ALBERT EINSTEIN

List

The only disability in life is a bad attitude.

SCOTT HAMILTON

We must all either wear out or rust out,
every one of us. My choice is to wear out.

THEODORE ROOSEVELT

ening

Seize the day, and put the least
possible trust in tomorrow.

HORACE

It's not whether you get knocked down;
it's whether you get up.

VINCE LOMBARDI

I don't know what I need to be ready for, but there is
evidently something. How strange if I lived all my life
doing things almost without wanting to, always feeling
that they were just a substitute for what I was really
meant to do and never finding what that was.

M.F.K. FISHER

One doesn't recognize in one's life the really
important moments—not until it's too late.

AGATHA CHRISTIE

Dream as if you'll live forever.
Live as if you'll die today.

JAMES DEAN

Do not dwell in the past, do not dwell in the future,
concentrate the mind on the present moment.

BUDDHA

Enjoy your ice-cream while it's on your plate,
that's my philosophy.

THORNTON WILDER

If I had my life to live over, I'd make the
same mistakes, only sooner.

TALLULAH BANKHEAD

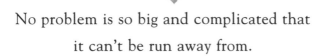

No problem is so big and complicated that
it can't be run away from.

CHARLES SCHULTZ

The world is full of cactus, but we don't have to sit on it.

WILL FOLEY

At the end of life, you will never regret not having passed one more test, not winning one more verdict, or not closing one more deal. You will regret time not spent with a husband, a child, a friend, or a parent.

BARBARA BUSH

Be more concerned with your character than with your reputation. Your character is what you really are while your reputation is merely what others think you are.

DALE CARNEGIE

I started with the firm conviction that when I came to the end, I wanted to be regretting the things that I *had* done, not the things I hadn't.

MICHAEL CAINE

A long life may not be good enough
but a good life is long enough.

BENJAMIN FRANKLIN

We learn the rope of life by untying its knots.

JEAN TOOMER

Let the world know you as you are,
not as you think you should be.

FANNY BRICE

The world is round and the place which may seem like
the end may also be only the beginning.

IVY BAKER PRIEST

There are no rehearsals in the symphony of life.

ANONYMOUS

61

Listen to the song of life.

KATHARINE HEPBURN

When your dreams turn to dust, vacuum.

DESMOND TUTU

To live content with small means; to seek elegance
rather than luxury, and refinement rather than fashion;
to be worthy, not respectable, and wealthy, not rich;
to study hard, think quietly, talk gently, act frankly;
to listen to stars and birds, to babes and sages, with open
heart; to bear all cheerfully, do all bravely, await occasions,
hurry never. In a word, to let the spiritual, unbidden and
unconscious, grow up through the common.

This is to be my symphony.

WILLIAM HENRY CHANNING

Happiness is not having what you want,
but wanting what you have.

HYMAN SCHACHTEL

The mindless renewal of nature each year—
it humbles you a little bit. And you realize the
best thing you can do is sprout your leaves again.

ARTHUR MILLER

I like trees because they seem more resigned to the way
they have to live than other things do.

WILLA CATHER

Happiness is not an elusive bird, perched high
near the ceiling, which, with the help of more or less
complicated ladders, you have to work to catch.
Happiness is an element, which, like air, is everywhere.

JACQUES HENRI LARTIGUE

If I didn't have spiritual faith, I would be a pessimist.
But I'm an optimist. I've read the last page in the Bible,
It's going to turn out all right.

BILLY GRAHAM

If every day is an awakening, you will never
grow old. You will just keep growing.

GAIL SHEEHY

I have a simple philosophy. Fill what's empty.
Empty what's full. Scratch where it itches.

ALICE ROOSEVELT LONGWORTH

No one gets out of this world alive, so the time to
live, learn, care, share, celebrate, and love is now.

LEO BUSCAGLIA

I am not afraid of tomorrow,
for I have seen yesterday and I love today.

WILLIAM ALLEN WHITE